Part 2: Four Empowering Lessons About Connection

TEXAS ANGEL PART 2

Beyond Blessed Assurance to Genuine Faith

Part 2: Four Empowering Lessons About Connection

INTENTIONAL | PURPOSEFUL | SOLUTIONS

DoGoodLeadership.me

Copyright © 2022 Do Good Enterprises, LLC
All rights reserved.

Part 2: Four Empowering Lessons About Connection

About the Author

I am Dr. Stephanie Duguid, daughter of the late Margie Rector. I am a wife, mom, daughter, sister, educator, friend, and leader.

My drive to share this comes from being raised by a strong, confident woman and more than 25 years in education as a teacher and administrator. I have been a lifelong educator with degrees in Human Performance, Sports Health Care, Curriculum and Instruction, and Educational Leadership. Through all my schooling and my life, I have had my mother as the driving force in my mind.

Now as a mom to two teenage boys that my mother never had the opportunity to meet, I strive to be a role model for them as my mother was to me! I want to be the one to show them how to be strong, confident, lead by example, and serve others.

Part 2: Four Empowering Lessons About Connection

I hope you enjoy this compilation of lessons learned by reflecting on the wonderful memories and interactions with my mom. By your purchase, you are contributing to a scholarship in my mother's name as well as helping others in need.

Thank you!

Part 2: Four Empowering Lessons About Connection

Special Information

I am glad you decided to be a part of the continuation of this story and helping others through your support by purchasing. Please be sure to read the forward where I share a reflection of how this book came to be. I hope you are as touched as I was living this journey.

Part 2: Four Empowering Lessons About Connection

One thing my mother always encouraged me to do was to follow my dreams. I am pursuing a personal goal of professional speaking, coaching, and training through Do Good Enterprises.

I would be honored if you would visit my website at: www.dogoodleadership.me

If you are interested in downloading a FREE Goal Setting Workbook, follow the link here: https://www.gp.dogoodleadership.me/optin

Part 2: Four Empowering Lessons About Connection

Dedication

I dedicate this to my mother, Marjorie. She is my guardian angel!

Part 2: Four Empowering Lessons About Connection

Contributions/Donations

My husband and I were honored to have the opportunity to create a scholarship in my mother's memory for those pursuing a degree in education, nursing, or social work that became endowed on February 2022 on the 82nd birthday of my mother. The hope is that her memorial scholarship will help those who share her passion for education, life of giving, and supporting those in need.

Therefore, a portion of the proceeds from each eBook will be donated to her memorial scholarship at Copiah-Lincoln Community College. If you would like to donate, please do so at: Give Now - Copiah-Lincoln Community College (colin.edu)

So, THANK YOU for being a part of the everlasting legacy for my mother, my angel in heaven!

Part 2: Four Empowering Lessons About Connection

Forward

We all have someone in our life that we look up to. That may be a teacher, a friend, a family member, or even a parent. For me, it was my mom!

I have enjoyed the foundation that my mother provided. She was my mom, a teacher, a friend, a church member, and a leader in the community. She led by example and touched so many.

This book is a continuation of the lessons learned from observing her actions. They were not written down or scripted along the way, they came about upon reflection and introspection after her passing.

Part 2: Four Empowering Lessons About Connection

I have found that certain themes have come about that were really modeled from her life, her giving, her service, and her spirit. I discovered that I have been told I honor her themes as well.

I hope you connect with the stories throughout, and the lessons learned. You will laugh, cry, feel love, and loss. But most of all, you will get a sense for what an amazing person she was.

Part 2: Four Empowering Lessons About Connection

Table of Contents

About the Author 3
Special Information 5
Dedication 7
Contributions/Donations 8
Forward 9
INTRODUCTION 13
LESSONS 15
Lesson 1: Care and Connection 17
Lesson 2: First Impressions 25
Lesson 3: The Impact of Words and Actions 31
Lesson 4: Leaving A Legacy 37
APPLICATION 45
Apply Lesson 1: Care and Connection 51
Apply Lesson 2: First Impressions 55
Apply Lesson 3: The Impact of Words and Actions 63
Apply Lesson 4: Leaving A Legacy 79
CONNECTION 89
COMMUNICATION 97
MY CHALLENGE TO YOU! 101

Part 2: Four Empowering Lessons About Connection

THANK YOU! 103

WHAT'S NEXT? 107

Part 2: Four Empowering Lessons About Connection

INTRODUCTION

I am writing this sentence on the 21st anniversary of my mom's passing. I have a hard time believing it has been 21 years since that phone call. Twenty-one years since I heard her voice. Twenty-one years since she has hugged me. Twenty-one years since I have seen her genuine smile.

But then I realize it has been 21 years of great memories. Twenty-one years of experiences that she was still a part of. Twenty-one years of love for her that helps to drive me each and every day.

In Texas Angel Part 1, I shared five essential life lessons. Be sure to read that book to really understand the entire story.

My mom's life and loss made me reflect and realize we can all learn from her. Although it was not planned, she

Part 2: Four Empowering Lessons About Connection

continued to be a teacher even in death. I would like to explore several thoughts emphasizing lessons learned.

As you read through each lesson, you will notice questions and a *reflection prompt* or *quote* at the end.

The questions help to think about your actions with others based on the lessons. Be honest with yourself when you answer.

The REFLECTION prompt or quote is meant to really look inside and see if you are connecting fully with others. See how you do!

Use the following page to *JOURNAL* your answers to the questions and the REFLECTION prompt or quote.

Part 2: Four Empowering Lessons About Connection

LESSONS

Part 2: Four Empowering Lessons About Connection

Part 2: Four Empowering Lessons About Connection

Lesson 1: Care and Connection

My mom was a force of nature. Not in a bad way, but in a friendly, always wearing bright colors, high heels, long nails, contagious smile, and laughing kind of way.

When mom came into a room or arrived somewhere fashionably late, as I explained in Texas Angel part one, you knew she was there. Everyone turned and looked at her. Everyone smiled! Everyone had an array of happiness in their eyes. Mom lit up the room.

When you interacted with her you were drawn to her smile, her kind words, her true intentionality to be present with you! She cared about you, who you were, your family, your job, career, kids, pets, current experiences, challenges, and it just continued. You felt like you were the center of attention and it felt good! Not in an interrogation way, but really felt like someone was interested in you.

Part 2: Four Empowering Lessons About Connection

She had that gift where people were just attracted to her. Like a moth to a flame, mom exuded genuine care and concern for others that would draw everyone to her.

As a teacher it was one of the best qualities she could have. Students loved her. They felt safe in her classroom, would really talk, and discuss things fully, and openly. They felt connected to her like family. That connection would not be a temporary feeling either like you have after eating a big bag of candy. This connection would last for hours, days, weeks, months, years, and for some, forever!

Mom had this natural charisma and memory where she could remember all her student's names, years after they were in her class. Mom taught about 150 students each semester for over 40 years. Simple math: 150 X 2=300, 300 X 40=12,000. That equation gives us over 12,000 students. That 12,000 is just at Dulles High School and only accounts for her students, not others

Part 2: Four Empowering Lessons About Connection

she got to know, those individuals at church, the community, or those friends and families associated with her children. Again, 12,000 students and she seemed to know, really know, every single one.

One student that connected with mom, like so many of her students, just felt comfortable. For many students, if there was a hole in the student's life, whether it was apparent, they would gravitate to her because she filled a void. She was present and cared. She completed that student!

One connected with my mom through similar personalities and they both were "bigger girls ". Some would call that "fluffy ".

Part 2: Four Empowering Lessons About Connection

No matter what some called it, positive or negative, my mom was confident in who she was and how she looked. She was a model for high school students struggling with their body image. Therefore, this student connected with mom and felt a sense of belonging while building her confidence. Mom cared about her students and this student really embraced that.

This student became one of the many students mom decided to help by providing opportunities to make a little extra money, and help mom at the same time.

Part 2: Four Empowering Lessons About Connection

Mom was not very computer savvy. She asked this student to digitize some personal files like notes, recipes, and much more.

Sadly, my mom passed away in the car accident soon thereafter and this student never got to finish the task of typing up the recipes. But this student didn't just throw them all away after mom's death. Because of the personal connection she had with my mom, she kept them close to her for many years. In fact, she kept them through several house moves, family changes, illnesses, and life events.

But just last year, this student decided to contact me after many phone calls through friends of friends. When we connected, she shared her personal story of how she and mom connected. She said she had all these family recipes that were mom's. I was shocked! I knew nothing about them. She graciously mailed them to me soon thereafter.

Part 2: Four Empowering Lessons About Connection

When I opened the box, I saw several manilla folders with mom's handwriting! It was like she was with me all over again.

These recipes were special! They had mom's name, my grandmother's name on mom's side, my dad's mom, his grandmother, and so on. There were hundreds of recipes from family and close friends. Every single person who had a recipe in this box had passed!

I felt compelled to share them all! I created a book of recipes entitled *Recipes from a Texas Angel in Heaven*. It is a compilation of 820 recipes covering more than 190 pages. Search for it on Amazon! Proceeds go to the Margie Rector Memorial Scholarship Fund at Copiah-Lincoln Community College!

Part 2: Four Empowering Lessons About Connection

Questions:
How do you show you care?
And to whom?
Do you expect something in return?
How often do you show you care?
How do you know they understand your caring message or gesture?
Do you need to do something different?
How?
When?

REFLECTION:

DO THOSE CLOSE TO ME KNOW THAT I CARE THROUGH MY DAILY ACTIONS?

Part 2: Four Empowering Lessons About Connection

JOURNAL:

Answers to the Questions:

_____
_____
_____
_____
_____
_____
_____
_____
_____
_____

Response to the REFLECTION:

_____
_____
_____
_____
_____
_____

Part 2: Four Empowering Lessons About Connection

Lesson 2: First Impressions

Each day mom greeted those around her with a smile. She was always happy, always confident, always kind, and always focused on you. Mom showed up every day for her students. She made every student feel like they mattered, that they were there for a reason, they had a purpose. Mom had a way of pulling the best out of her students, making them grow and develop in ways they never thought possible. She made them shift away from their comfort zone and explore possibilities.

Part 2: Four Empowering Lessons About Connection

Her daily actions elicited high expectations in a loving respectful manner and gave students the confidence and desire to continue to develop themselves. She didn't have favorites or only do for one or two students, she did this for everyone she encountered. She would draw the best out of you, and the way she did it made students love her, respect her, appreciate her.

That feeling would stay with them long after they were in Mrs. Rector's class, long after high school and even into their adult lives. The positive impact in her classes at Dulles High School influenced their entire life to find the good, be your best, and stretch beyond your limits to reach towards your goals.

Impact and Influence!

Over the years, mom had a lot of practice greeting people. It started when she was in a sorority at Northwestern University, continued as a Welcome Wagon lady in Sugar Land, and into the classroom at

Part 2: Four Empowering Lessons About Connection

Dulles High School. She was always the greeter. She loved to have gatherings where people came together to talk, interact, mingle, and get to know one another.

Mom made the best first impression. She was happy, smiling, positive, and you felt amazing too. We can all learn from her. You can never get another first impression, so make it the best one ever.

Think about the term *First Impression*. The term itself means the primary effect, feeling, or image retained because of an experience according to American Heritage Dictionary.

When we have an initial interaction with someone, we quickly survey their face and facial expressions, voice inflection, general emotional state, and how the person is dressed, attractiveness, and posture. If you think about it, it is hard to think of anyone differently once you have that first impression.

Part 2: Four Empowering Lessons About Connection

According to Psychology Today, it takes seven seconds to make a first impression. First impressions are important because they can make you seem trustworthy, help you make friends more easily, they can make or break a potential relationship, they help you go farther in your goals, and they boost self-esteem.

Upon reflection of my mom, she met all the criteria of a good first impression! She was friendly which comes through as trustworthiness, she had many friends, she was able to develop relationships with almost everyone she met, she was successful as a teacher, in church, and in the community, and she had great self-esteem.

We can all learn from her actions, her interactions, her demeanor, and her positive aura!

Part 2: Four Empowering Lessons About Connection

Questions:
Reflect on a memorable first impression.
What made that interaction stand out?
Was it positive or negative?
What do people say about your first impression?
How do you know?

REFLECTION:

AM I PURPOSEFUL IN MY INTERACTIONS WITH THE INTENT OF FOCUSING ON THE POSITIVE?

Part 2: Four Empowering Lessons About Connection

JOURNAL:

Answers to the Questions:

Response to the REFLECTION:

Part 2: Four Empowering Lessons About Connection

Lesson 3: The Impact of Words and Actions

Consistency

Mom was very genuine. She didn't fake her happiness or her caring nature, her optimism, and rose-colored glasses attitude. That was REAL! She truly DID care for those around her. She WAS interested in what you had to say, and she LISTENED intently to each word.

Mom was a GREAT communicator. She knew how to speak to people, what to say, and knew that body language mattered. Let me explain.

Let's begin with how she spoke clearly, without unnecessary pauses (um, you know, and), always formed her words, and did not mumble or fidget. She used appropriate words for her audience whether it was a little girl at church, a student or the principal at

Part 2: Four Empowering Lessons About Connection

school, or the Texas senator in Washington D.C., she knew how to speak.

Mom was also a pro at body language, 70% of communication. She never crossed her arms, always had her feet toward you, and had great eye contact and facial expression. She even reached out and touched you on the arm or hand at the appropriate times.

Mom was always the same. You knew what you were going to get each time you encountered her. This big ball of energy exuding positivity, care, concern, and genuine interest. She was CONSISTENT.

Part 2: Four Empowering Lessons About Connection

For many students, mom was the most consistent thing they had. Mom taught school in the 60's, 70's, 80's, and 90's. This was before many conditions like mental and emotional health challenges were formerly diagnosed. This was before people openly talked about struggles. When you had to cope with many things yourself including love, loss, divorce, death, and abuse. However, mom was there for her students. She was consistent, present, and a confident woman, teacher, and mom. Students fled to her so easily. They loved her!

Her consistency was one thing in life they could count on. When everything else around them seemed to be falling apart, they could count on Mrs. Rector at Dulles High School. She would show up. She was their rock.

Part 2: Four Empowering Lessons About Connection

Questions:
Have you ever had someone tell you that you matter?
That you are important?
That you made a difference in their life?
As you reflect on that moment, did you plan your interaction?
Was it scripted or did it just happen?

REFLECTION:

YOU NEVER REALLY KNOW THE TRUE IMPACT YOU HAVE ON THOSE AROUND YOU. YOU NEVER KNOW HOW MUCH SOMEONE NEEDED THAT SMILE YOU GAVE THEM. YOU NEVER KNOW HOW YOUR KINDNESS TURNED SOMEONE'S ENTIRE LIFE AROUND. YOU NEVER KNOW HOW MUCH SOMEONE NEEDED THAT LONG HUG OR DEEP TALK. SO DON'T WAIT TO BE KIND. DON'T WAIT FOR SOMEONE ELSE TO BE KIND FIRST. DON'T WAIT FOR BETTER CIRCUMSTANCES OR FOR SOMEONE TO CHANGE. JUST BE KIND, BECAUSE YOU NEVER KNOW HOW MUCH SOMEONE NEEDS IT.

~NIKKI BANAS

Part 2: Four Empowering Lessons About Connection

JOURNAL:

Answers to the Questions:

_____
_____
_____
_____
_____
_____
_____
_____
_____
_____

Response to the REFLECTION:

_____
_____
_____
_____
_____
_____

Part 2: Four Empowering Lessons About Connection

Part 2: Four Empowering Lessons About Connection

Lesson 4: Leaving A Legacy

The Ability to Still Comfort Those Based on Memories

My mom was a teacher, but not just to her students at Dulles, she was a teacher to everyone, all the time, including those in the community, to strangers. Mom taught lessons with every interaction, every encounter, every day.

Mom led by example. She was kind, caring, and compassionate. No matter your station in life, she treated you with genuine respect. She practiced the *Golden Rule*, "Do unto others as you would want them to do unto you". She was present in her moment, and she worked to serve others. She was a force of nature.

Mom also had a hilarious side to her and a contagious laugh. She was just funny and silly. She would do things that would *stick* in your mind forever. Now we say, "that was mom".

Part 2: Four Empowering Lessons About Connection

Mom left a legacy through her actions and the way she made those around her feel. But she also left some amazing memories that are triggered through daily experiences: a word, phrase, a song, a smell, and plenty of memories.

Let me share two stories:

Volleyball Dress

You have heard me say that my mother was a teacher at Dulles High School. What you do not yet know is that Dulles High School is the rival to the school I attended, Clements High School. We were in the same district

Part 2: Four Empowering Lessons About Connection

and always had fierce competitions in any athletic event.

I happened to play volleyball for Clements High School. And when Clements and Dulles played, my mom would of course cheer for me, but she also cheered for her team. She was "torn" between the two. In fact, my mom had a special dress made for that occasion.

The dress had a dividing line down the middle with one side red with a blue stripe, and the other blue with a red stripe. She had volleyballs on each side with the names of each school as well.

Part 2: Four Empowering Lessons About Connection

She would sit in the middle of the bleachers at the top so that she was supporting both teams!

That dress is just one example of the lengths mom went to connect and support those around her.

Big Hair, Closer to God

I have shared many times that mom was the typical Texas woman with big hair, an enormous smile, long nails, high heels, and a personality to match.

Mom was known for her hair. But people didn't make fun of her or joke about her. They truly thought it fit all that she was in life! Mom was a Christian woman who served in the church and in the community.

So, as she got older, her coarse blond hair shifted from a short hairstyle that eventually grew to touch her shoulders, to a large puffy helmet that reflected light like the sun. As she got older, her helmet only grew larger.

Part 2: Four Empowering Lessons About Connection

She always joked that she was simply getting closer with God!

Part 2: Four Empowering Lessons About Connection

Questions:
Have you ever had memories of someone that were so vivid that you felt you were replaying history?
Have you ever had a memory that made you smile?
Made you feel loved?
Embrace that feeling!

REFLECTION:

WHAT CAN I DO TODAY TO SERVE OTHERS? HOW CAN I LIVE TODAY AND BE PROUD OF THE PERSON I AM AFTER I AM GONE?

Part 2: Four Empowering Lessons About Connection

JOURNAL:

Answers to the Questions:

_____
_____
_____
_____
_____
_____
_____
_____
_____
_____

Response to the REFLECTION:

_____
_____
_____
_____
_____
_____

Part 2: Four Empowering Lessons About Connection

Part 2: Four Empowering Lessons About Connection

APPLICATION

How Have I Taken the Four Empowering Lessons About Connection and Applied Then in My Life?

Those four lessons are what I have drawn from mom's life and how she influenced others. But truly, she directly influenced me.

They say the apple doesn't fall far from the tree. In regular terms that means that kids are a very strong reflection of their parents.

When I was growing up, mom often embarrassed me. Remember those stories I was sharing earlier?

I was reserved, a bit of an introvert, liked Earth tone colors, did not wear heels, played sports so long nails were not an option, wore minimal makeup (comparatively), and my hair was long and straight. And I was always early if I had my choice.

Part 2: Four Empowering Lessons About Connection

But mom was the opposite. She was loud, colorful, and always late. But she was kind, considerate, and caring.

I guess the apple is similar, but not the same. I still wear Earth tones and calm colors (usually professional black

Part 2: Four Empowering Lessons About Connection

pants), have somewhat straight hair, and am calm when I enter a room.

But I AM positive, optimistic, caring, know how to communicate, and serve others. I still don't wear heels and am on time for everything, usually very early.

But over time, I have started to wear darker lipstick, my hair has become wavy (after having my kids), thicker (I must get it thinned) and coarser. So, it is a lot of hair, and in Mississippi humidity, sometimes "big". When I enter a room, it is done with confidence and certainty, not through "announcements" and exhibited energy.

So, you could say I am like my mom through education and positivity.

- **Education:** I LOVE going to school to learn new things! I am also a teacher and administrator in education.
- **Positivity "Do Good"**: I have a positive influence and outlook just as she did! I also started a

Part 2: Four Empowering Lessons About Connection

company called Do Good Enterprises to share positivity, motivation, and inspiration!

On Facebook, many friends and former students have positive memories of mom! They share stories and comments with me on a regular basis. And even my son Dalton, who has NEVER met her, is so much like my mom. He is empathetic, very caring, and Godlike in his mannerism. *(Read Texas Angel Part 1 for the rest of the story about the connection between my mother and my son Dalton).*

In fact, I am honored my other was around for much of my early years and was even present at my wedding! My fiancé (now husband) and I decided to semi-elope to South Lake Tahoe to get married. We had a total of 13 people present which included us! With family and friends living across multiple states, we decided this would be the simplest and most logical option!

Part 2: Four Empowering Lessons About Connection

But sadly, my mother never did have the chance to meet my boys. Below is the picture of the first time they met her at the cemetery!

Part 2: Four Empowering Lessons About Connection

Part 2: Four Empowering Lessons About Connection

Apply Lesson 1: Care and Connection

How do YOU show you care? Do you give tangible things to show you care or do you promise to be present? Care can be *seen* in many ways. Some think it is items received, others prefer the feel and touch of a hand or a hug. Others see it in gestures like cleaning the house, making a meal, or holding a door. Yet others see it in a smile, wink, or other non-verbal manner. I see it in all those ways.

The main goal is to think of others, move from self-ISH to self-LESS. For some that quality is present early on as a child. For others, it is learned, and for some, it never happens.

I choose to see the needs, wants, and desires of others. When you serve others and show you care, you yourself

Part 2: Four Empowering Lessons About Connection

begin to feel honored, elated, and confident in who you are.

As you live your life each day, are you so focused on yourself that you do not notice the world around you? Or are you someone who is observant, caring, courteous, helpful, and encouraging. Are you willing to stop and help a friend or neighbor, are you willing to listen to a colleague or your own child, are you willing to go out of your way to help someone else?

I encourage you to smile more, laugh often, call someone just because, or write a handwritten note! You can also send a text, write an email, or send them a selfie to let them know you are thinking of them!

If you take just a moment, you can change their entire day, week, month, or even year!

I have had a few friends recently that had terrible life events. Whether it was a divorce, death in the family,

Part 2: Four Empowering Lessons About Connection

cancer, or another ailment, they simply needed to know that someone is thinking of them and cares for them.

I would make intentional efforts to check in via text every couple of days, send a card, or just listen when they needed a friend to talk to. Giving of yourself and your time is so impactful.

Within the past year, I was sick along with the rest of the family (and the world at that time). I was struggling to take care of myself, much less my family. I had some amazing friends that would come check on us all, bring food for meals, and would even take my kids to all their school events. I didn't ask them to, they simply offered. They didn't expect anything in return, but I was forever grateful!

Take time to show someone you care and connect!

Part 2: Four Empowering Lessons About Connection

Part 2: Four Empowering Lessons About Connection

Apply Lesson 2: First Impressions

Think of your own first impression. Either your first impression of someone else, or the first impression someone had of you.

When I think of the term first impression, I usually think about what others think and feel when we meet for the first time. I realize that my demeanor, my attitude, and my aura is all seen and felt by those around me. If I am negative, grumpy, and agitated, others see and feel that and most likely avoid me. But if I am smiling, open, jovial, then people are drawn to me. I choose the latter.

I try to smile often, be approachable, and listen to those I encounter. I remember that what I am seeing, thinking, experiencing personally is ME. I should not take it, whatever it is, out on someone new. The first interaction sets the foundation for all others…make it a positive one.

Part 2: Four Empowering Lessons About Connection

If you have ever been to school, grade school, high school, college, and beyond, you probably remember some first impressions you had of your teachers.

I remember my 7th grade honors math teacher. I don't remember her name, but I remember her!! She was petite, was tidy with blonde hair pulled back tightly in a perfectly shaped bun and had round plastic glasses precisely on her nose. She wore a skirt and a jacket that were off white in color that laid perfectly on her body.

Part 2: Four Empowering Lessons About Connection

She sat next to the overhead projector with her legs crossed and "told" you what to do. There was no conversation, no emotion, no connection, nothing! I was just in a room with 25 other kids and felt nothing! I hated this class. I despised it! I couldn't learn a thing in there. She didn't care. She didn't have any sense of what the students were experiencing. It was awful.

I told my mom that I was struggling, and I was soon moved to the next level of math class down the hall. The first day I entered the room I was nervous. But then the teacher came to me, made eye contact with me, welcomed me to the class, put her hand on my shoulder and focused on me. Wow! We connected! She led me to my desk, showed me the page in my textbook, and confirmed I was ready. Then she walked to the front of the room, turned, smiled, and winked at the class, but I felt it was a sign she was glad I was there, and continued the lesson.

Part 2: Four Empowering Lessons About Connection

That year I learned to LOVE math. And it all started with a first impression.

So, as you go about your day, remember that whatever is going on in your own personal world, someone new has no knowledge or understanding of it. Use your first impression, first interaction, first opportunity as one to positively connect through eye contact, body language, voice tone, and a smile. You never get a second chance at a first impression.

Several factors influence your first impression of someone (and even yourself) including nonverbal communication or body language, physical features, clothing, accessories, and hairstyle, voice or speech, and the surrounding environment.

Many times, we do not even stop to think about the impression we are about to make. We do not consciously prepare for each and every interaction we have. But we must realize that we leave an impression

Part 2: Four Empowering Lessons About Connection

on each person we meet. So how can we leave the most favorable first impression possible?

There are several things we can do! Stay conscious of your body language. Body language is most of our means of communication. Be sure to open your posture, make eye contact, listen actively, and avoid fidgeting.

It is also essential that you show your interest. Remember, everything is NOT about YOU! Express interest and enthusiasm in someone that is speaking to you. Be sure to ask a thoughtful question showing that you are paying attention. Do not be that person that is so busy thinking of a response, that you forget to listen to the conversation.

Be sure to check your facial expressions. I bought a sign for a colleague that said, "I'm sorry, did I roll my eyes out loud?" Facial expressions matter. Those that laugh, smile, and show excitement tend to have better first impressions. And those that are angry, frustrated, or

Part 2: Four Empowering Lessons About Connection

experiencing other negative emotions must be cautious not to exude those emotions towards those around you, especially if you are trying to make a favorable first impression.

Always dress for the occasion. If you are going to a job interview, it is best to have the appropriate business attire on rather than loungewear. If you are at an event for your preferred interest or hobby, be sure to dress the part. Dress is not the most important factor in a first impression, but it is a big part.

Of course, your language can impact your first impression. Things you may say to your best friend when you are at a restaurant may differ from what you say to your parents, teachers, or supervisor. Think before you speak is always a good rule of thumb.

The bottom line is that most of what we experience during a first impression is largely unconscious. In short, we cannot always control them. If that is the case, then many may ask, why bother?

Part 2: Four Empowering Lessons About Connection

I encourage you to approach EVERY new interaction with kindness, empathy, and a willingness to learn and grow. That is what my mother did when she connected so well with those around her. We can all do the same!

Part 2: Four Empowering Lessons About Connection

Part 2: Four Empowering Lessons About Connection

Apply Lesson 3: The Impact of Words and Actions

In my own life, I have done many things for my career. I was an athletic trainer, a K-12 teacher, a college teacher, and now a college administrator. I am also a wife, mom, daughter, and sister.

In my world now, I always say I am not doing my daily work or actions for me. I do it for the instructors and students, as I am here to serve them. But my focus remains on the students. Without students we don't have a college. And everything in between is to support students; their learning, their development and growth, and their educational journey.

As an administrator, I must make, what faculty say, are the hard decisions. Of course, there are management decisions such as schedules, paperwork, employee absences, navigating facilities, and daily activities too.

Part 2: Four Empowering Lessons About Connection

But the other part is holding students accountable. At the college level, there are expectations, policies, and procedures that must be followed for the entire system to be functional and flow. I must hold students accountable when they don't meet expectations. In having the conversations with students, no matter what the challenge is, I am consistent. I focus on being consistent. Of course, I welcome students into my office and listen to their side of the story, but I also have done my part to gather information and know more details than they do most likely. No matter what it is, I follow policy, I discuss expectations, what was and was not met, and then a decision is made for the next step.

In most cases, the student leaves my office knowing they have a voice. They understand the outcome, and they understand why it ended as it did. Although they may not like the decision, they understand.

The faculty make a point to thank me for being supportive and consistent day in and day out. They

Part 2: Four Empowering Lessons About Connection

know that if a student is sent to me, the issue will be handled fairly, consistently, and calmly. They also know I will follow up and share the outcome.

We are a team! A team that helps support each other working toward a similar goal…guiding students along their educational journey so they can lead successful lives to contribute to society and support their families.

Let me share a few student experiences!

Part 2: Four Empowering Lessons About Connection

Actions influence others

Student #1

I had a non-traditional student come see me a few years ago. That means the student was not the typical 18–20-year-old. She was a mature wife, mom, and friend who was trying to finish all her classes to reach her lifelong dream of earning a degree. But on this day, she looked defeated. With sadness in her eyes, she walked in my office and said "I can't do this! I am not going to finish my classes this semester. I have to quit." When I invited her in for a conversation, she began to share all her struggles, sources of stress, and concern.

She was a single mom with a severely disabled special needs son. She worked two jobs to support her entire family and had extra challenges because of her son's needs. She said she had been trying to finish her degree to better her life and show her family she could do it. A degree would also help provide for her family with a better job, but she just didn't think she could do

Part 2: Four Empowering Lessons About Connection

it. Not today! She ultimately felt she had too many classes left and could not be successful.

She felt the journey was too long. She could not commit to her studies, and she just needed to quit.

This student had been going to school part-time which translates to one or two classes each semester. To complete an associate degree (60 hours), that means it would take five or more years at that rate. She also wanted to take classes face to face in a classroom and not online. So, her commitment also included specific dates, travel time, parking, interactions, and traffic. She was simply overwhelmed.

I really listened to her struggles and in a soft voice, I said, "well, let's look at your progress. Let me take a few moments and evaluate your unofficial transcript and see where you are". She agreed.

Part 2: Four Empowering Lessons About Connection

By this time, she was just sitting in a chair across from me with tears in her eyes, head down, bent over with such a defeated posture. She was fidgeting with a tissue in her hand. She looked like she felt broken.

I finished the evaluation and looked up at her and smiled.

I said, "I want you to know how far you have come. If you successfully finish the two classes you have now, you have only three more to complete your degree."

She immediately looked at me and said, "What?". I continued, "if you complete those two classes you are in now, take two classes in the spring, and one in the summer, you can graduate!"

She was in disbelief. Her jaw dropped open, and she stared at me.

I said, "You CAN do this! I know this has been your dream and you are almost there! YOU...CAN...DO...THIS!"

Part 2: Four Empowering Lessons About Connection

We sat and talked about the specific classes needed and developed a plan. We talked about the challenges and arrangements outside of the classroom she had to navigate to make this work.

Her defeated posture turned into an upright one with hope in her eyes and a smile beaming across her face. Her tears were now tears of excitement and disbelief.

When we finished our conversation, she came around the desk and gave me a hug and said, "THANK YOU!"

We parted ways, but I would soon hear from her again!

At the December graduation (we didn't have one in August) I was walking around congratulating all the graduates. I embraced their smiles, their excitement their radiance of confidence. One of the graduates was this student. She ran to me and said, "I DID IT!"

She continued to tell me that I was the reason she was there. She had planned to quit that day during the previous fall term, but said that my compassion,

Part 2: Four Empowering Lessons About Connection

empathy, willingness to evaluate her situation, and the kind and respectful conversation made her feel special, important, like I cared. She gave ME credit for her success. I was touched, honored, and had chills. But we all know SHE is the hero in here!

The story doesn't stop there. This student was now on a mission. She had conquered her first dream and embraced the confidence to push herself further. She continued to the university and completed her bachelors. When she finished, she made a point to call me and share the great news. We celebrated together on the phone, and I told her I was so proud of her.

Soon thereafter, I received another call from her. This time it was a request to be a reference for her application to a master's program. You heard me, a master's program.

This student's life changed in my office. From our single conversation demonstrating kindness, caring, empathy,

Part 2: Four Empowering Lessons About Connection

listening, and a real conversation, her life changed…. forever!!!

That is one of many stories about a single moment, a catalyst, that changes everything. We never know how our words and actions may affect those around us. But if we are truly engaged, optimistic, intentional, and purposeful, great things can happen.

***

Now, I don't go out and look for these life changing situations. It doesn't happen that way. But rather if you live life the best way you can, are consistent in your persistence, interactions, and genuine in your actions, you will be amazed. Positive breeds positive.

Student #2

I was going to check on a class of an instructor that called in sick and came across a student in the dark. As I entered the room, I heartily asked the student, after I said, good morning, "Did you see the announcement in

Part 2: Four Empowering Lessons About Connection

Canvas?" (That is our Learning Management System for our students). He said he was just downloading it as he was fidgeting with his phone.

The student then looked up at me and said, "Do you remember me?" Now, I get asked that all the time. And I am not like my mom where I remember everyone's name. But this student, I DID remember his face, but not his name, and I shared that! He continued to say, "You are the reason I am here, the reason I am in this room, the reason I am in school." I paused and said, "I am?" He continued and said, "yes, that day at registration, I didn't know what I wanted to do, and you took the time to talk to me, answer my questions, and had such a positive outlook that made me want to be here". I admit, that gave me chills. I was so happy for this young man. I was just doing and living the way I do day in and day out and connected with him.

A few days later he was back in my office. His work schedule did not merge with his current school schedule

Part 2: Four Empowering Lessons About Connection

and additional extracurricular commitment. We sat in my office talking about options, adjusting, and looking at the future. I told him that he needed to check in every couple of weeks so I could help answer any questions, direct him when he was lost, and help nudge him toward his goals. He was very appreciative of my time and said I made him feel important...That is why I am here.

Students come to my office all the time. As the Dean of Academics, I work to keep the instructional area progressive, functional, and moving in a positive direction through daily trouble shooting and goal planning. But daily, I also have students that come in and out of my office with varying questions and issues. And each day, I welcome them in, listen, have a conversation, and we both smile when they leave.

Faculty are no different. They too come to me with questions, challenges, frustrations, celebrations, and sometimes disbelief. I approach faculty the same way-

Part 2: Four Empowering Lessons About Connection

welcome them in, listen, have a conversation, and we both smile when they leave.

Faculty

But with faculty, many also come in to complain. Complaining about the AC, complaining about the water leak, complaining about a software, complaining about a schedule, a student, the purpose of a meeting, or sometimes just to complain. The biggest challenge is they usually come to me and expect me to fix whatever it is they are complaining about. Unfortunately, those that complain do so about issues I cannot control. I cannot control mother nature, facilities, or college policies. I cannot control what others say or how those words made them feel. But I can control our interaction, outlook, and optimism.

I had a challenge that I shared at the beginning of this year's Faculty Meeting. *Stay Positive and Be Kind*.

Part 2: Four Empowering Lessons About Connection

This is the actual sign hanging on my door at work.

My challenge was to FIND THE GOOD in situations and remain kind to those around you. It didn't stop there. I also shared with faculty that there would be no more complaining. I shared that if they did have a complaint that they also had to come with a solution. This was a practice encouraged by the Power of Positive Leadership author Jon Gordon. I wanted faculty to have some responsibility in thinking of how to change an outcome, think critically, and ask questions.

From that initiative, I was pleasantly surprised; many faculty approached me and said, "thank you!". So many were getting tired of the complaints, but they didn't

Part 2: Four Empowering Lessons About Connection

know what to do. They were feeling suffocated by the FEW that complained about everything. This expectation lifted a weight off their shoulders. It gave them an outlet and a voice. If a complainer started complaining to them, they would point to the challenge of *Stay Positive and Be Kind* and guide them to the process of submitting a solution.

The next year, this portion of the challenge stayed. However, I added to it. Now I encouraged everyone to be still, think about their why, really look inside, and reflect. Why are they here? Does their WHY align with what they are doing, how they are living for their passion in life? I challenged them to become aligned, work toward making sure they wanted to be here, they enjoyed being here, and they had a purpose and passion to be here.

So many times, we get caught up in daily activities, caught in the cycle of a schedule, meetings, answering

Part 2: Four Empowering Lessons About Connection

to others, daily tasks, and navigating life that we lose ourselves and forget our why.

After that challenge, I received more compliments, more assurance, and more thanks than ever before. Faculty appreciated the continued focus on positivity, but they appreciated the honesty, focus, guidance, presence, and challenge to find themselves.

Others come to me thankful for my consistency. Consistency with my actions, my attitude, my demeanor, and my decisions. They say they fully trust my intent and know I am true to my word, honest, follow protocol, and fully support them. One continued to email me and thank me for always supporting faculty and leading by example.

All those qualities I learned from my mom. I watched her with students, other teachers, administrators, church members, and the community. She too was positive, optimistic, consistent, caring, and present.

Part 2: Four Empowering Lessons About Connection

Part 2: Four Empowering Lessons About Connection

Apply Lesson 4: Leaving A Legacy

I don't know about you, but as I live each day, there are often "triggers" that remind me of mom. It could be a view of a ceramic apple she used to keep on her desk, the ring sitting proudly in my jewelry box she used to wear, the cross hanging in my hallway she used to pray to, or the Sandi Patti song she used to sing to. Other times it is the memory of events that made me laugh.

When mom came to visit us in Phoenix for the weekend, she brought not one suitcase, but two. One had her clothes and toiletries, and the second contained papers and cards. Now you might be thinking they were some sort of family legacy, or refer to historical excitement, or maybe even something she had written. No, you would be off base. This suitcase was filled with contents from a file cabinet mom wanted to clean out.

What?

Part 2: Four Empowering Lessons About Connection

She had packed a suitcase with the weight of paper, files, cards, and put them on a plane, flew them from Houston to Phoenix, over a three-day weekend, so she could clean out her file cabinet?

Her justification was that she knew she would have some quiet time to sit and focus, uninterrupted, to go through the contents….and she did.

That is also the trip where she sat in our backyard and admired the sunset and enjoyed the desert air. She loved animals and tried to call our cat over to jump into her lap. But the outdoor white cat just sat there and looked at her. Mom called, "Princess, come here!" in her loving voice while moving her fingers to entice the cat. But each time she called "Princess" the cat just stared. A while later, mom came into the house just frustrated. She could not believe I had an adult cat that didn't know her name and could not come when called. I said, what do you mean? She said, "Princess does not

Part 2: Four Empowering Lessons About Connection

know her name!!!". I just smiled and laughed, "Of course, not mom, because her name is Duchess!!"

We both looked at each other and could not contain the laughter. We had tears rolling down our cheeks. Mom knew it was a name of royalty but had selected the wrong one.

***

I have mentioned mom was a teacher a time or two. As a teacher, there are items you always have around. Things like pens, pencils, Manilla folders, staples, paperclips, notebooks, chalk, post-it notes, and other consumable office supplies

I found school supplies in every corner of her classroom, our home, and even her car. We were surrounded. She loved school and office supplies. To put this into perspective, when my mom died in 2001, I found boxes of paper clips and staples throughout her house. So many, in fact, that I have, just this year, 2022, gone

Part 2: Four Empowering Lessons About Connection

through the last box of staples with one more box of paper clips remaining. You may be saying "Great, what's the big deal?" The big deal is that at the writing of this book, it has been 21 years after her passing. Mom had 21 years' worth of office supplies stashed in her house. You are probably thinking that I just forgot about them and recently found the supplies to use.

Nope! Not the case. I too am in education. My husband is an educator. My 2 boys are students in junior high and high school. And we use her supplies on a regular basis. My mom had boxes of school supplies. Using paper clips and staples reminds me of her. We use her supplies every day. Twenty-one years' worth of supplies!

***

Mom also had a love of mirrors. Not in the vanity way, but she loved the light they reflected. Loved the shine of them. Loved that they made spaces feel grander,

Part 2: Four Empowering Lessons About Connection

loved the illusion of a different perspective, but also loved that she could put her lipstick on in every room.

If you look at many of her pictures, mirrors were in the background. Hanging on walls, sitting on tables like coasters, framed on a tabletop, or covering entire walls. Mom loved them. In fact, each time I see a mirror, I think of her and so do other family members.

When mom died, the oldest girl cousin specifically asked to have a mirror from mom's home as it reminded her of my mom. I thought it was just me.

Part 2: Four Empowering Lessons About Connection

The mirrors were also a place where you didn't feel alone. When you stood in front of them, someone was right there looking back. Not in a creepy, horror film kind of way, but in an assuring, you are not alone kind of way. You could see your own reflection. You could literally "reflect" and think and dream. Is the person I am "seeing" the person I want to be? Am I "reflecting" the strength, the confidence, the vision I want to exude? If not, what do I need to work on? Is it my posture? My facial expression? My general demeanor?

A mirror to most is just a mirror. But to mom, it was a "reflection" device and a friend. By taking a few minutes you could really see yourself, and the vision that others saw as well. It can allow you to see the image others see.

***

My mom also loved purses, and like most women, high heeled shoes, bright lipstick, and long nails. But she also loved sunglasses. She had sunglasses everywhere.

Part 2: Four Empowering Lessons About Connection

In her purse, in the glove box in the car, in the trunk, on the desk, in the kitchen drawer, on her nightstand and on the table as you walked out the door. THEY WERE EVERYWHERE. When you think of sunglasses, you may be thinking of aviators, or delicately framed petit lenses to go with each outfit. No! Mom had large framed, pink, or purple oversized sunglasses.

The type she would stack over other reading glasses before transition lenses were a thing. She thought she

Part 2: Four Empowering Lessons About Connection

was so smart to buy sunglasses that would fit over her reading glasses. I am smiling as I am writing this at the memory of her. The funny thing is that, at the time, no one else did this, but everyone who saw mom with double layers of glasses thought it was normal for her. She pulled it off. People didn't see a crazy woman who wore two pairs of glasses outside. They saw her happiness, jovial expression, bright smile, and confidence. And the double glasses were just part of that!

This is a picture of my mom, my older sister, and me with a pair of sunglasses on to match mom.

Part 2: Four Empowering Lessons About Connection

Recently I had to get new glasses. As I was looking for the perfect functional frame, in my gaze across the room, I saw mom's glasses. Well, not HER actual glasses, but the pair that reminded me of her. I could not resist. No, I didn't buy them, but I did try them on.

As soon as I did, they made me smile! Not just a facial smile, but a whole body, positive feeling, slight giggle kind of smile. Her memory makes me happy.

Part 2: Four Empowering Lessons About Connection

Part 2: Four Empowering Lessons About Connection

CONNECTION

Why write this book about a Texas Angel, my mom?

Two books really. Memories Shared!

Well, it all comes down to the influence she had on me and the influence I see she had on others. You see, when I was growing up in Sugar Land, Texas, it was a small town where we would ride our bikes anywhere. We didn't have cell phones, no GPS trackers, no Internet, no digital games, no interactive software, and no social media. We had to talk, communicate, interact, and also trust one another every day. You really had to get to know one another by speaking, using body language, and nonverbal cues, and write things with pen and paper or use a typewriter (some may ask what that is?)

Part 2: Four Empowering Lessons About Connection

Through all those interactions you had to grow, develop, and learn to be social. And my mom was a pro. She wasn't perfect all the time, but I chose to remember the positive interactions and memories.

Mom was a talker. She talked to me at home, talked to students at school, talked to friends on the phone, talked to neighbors outside, made a point to connect with friends and family often by calling or writing handwritten notes! She was a connector.

Every time I would speak to one of my friends or one of her former students, they would always say "I remember your mom". Then they would continue with "She was *(a happy memory)*" or "She always made me feel *(something positive)*", or "She taught me *(something great)*", or "I will always remember *(the time...)*". It was all positive and they were always smiling.

With social media, when I connect with someone new, they ALWAYS say the same thing! She was a positive

Part 2: Four Empowering Lessons About Connection

force that made so many feel good, feel important, feel loved. She was able to connect, not just share contact information and drop an e-mail later, but truly connect where she created lasting relationships and memories for so many.

Therefore, I wanted to share her principles of connection. I wanted to show others what true connection really looks like and how it is expressed.

***

Why connect? What are the benefits? If you Google "The Benefit of Connection", you will find many responses. General feedback will include:

#1: It is good for mental health

#2: It increases fulfillment

#3: It increases lifespan in years

#4: It improves your quality of life

Part 2: Four Empowering Lessons About Connection

But beyond what Google or any other scholarly resource says, why do you think connecting has benefits?

Think about how you feel when you see someone for the first time in years, or an old elementary school friend requests you on Facebook, Instagram, Snapchat, or any other social media outlets. How do you react? Remember we are focusing on the *positive*.

Here are some pictures from the past that make me smile. I am smiling because of the picture itself, but also because of the memories that come with the picture, the setting, the people there in the background, the experience.

Part 2: Four Empowering Lessons About Connection

You probably smile, your face may light up, it may trigger memories, it may make your heart flutter or give you chills. Connections matter! Connections are important. If you have those positive responses every time you connect think of the positive long-term benefits connecting, just from an anatomical standpoint.

Part 2: Four Empowering Lessons About Connection

- Reduces your stress level
- your endorphin levels kick in which means feel good you take deep breaths you set up an improved posture
- your blood pressure decreases
- your body posture is positive

Connection and communication are key, and GREAT for your health!

Questions:
Am I truly making connections with others?
How can I make one more connection today?

Part 2: Four Empowering Lessons About Connection

JOURNAL:

Answers to the Questions:

_____
_____
_____
_____
_____
_____
_____
_____
_____
_____
_____
_____
_____
_____
_____
_____
_____
_____
_____

Part 2: Four Empowering Lessons About Connection

Part 2: Four Empowering Lessons About Connection

COMMUNICATION

When I say communication, many quickly think about talking. By talking we are communicating. Well, let's think about that. When we say talking what does that mean?

To me that means two people speaking to one another in the same room, looking at each other, exchanging messages, displaying non-verbal cues through body language back and forth like waves. Others think talking means texting, emailing, Facebook messaging, sending emojis, using other social media outlets, or just body language like a thumbs up, a wink, a nod, or some other bat signal.

So, if the word *talking* when it comes to communication has many different meanings, think about the entire process of communication. It is extremely complex! Let me explain...

Part 2: Four Empowering Lessons About Connection

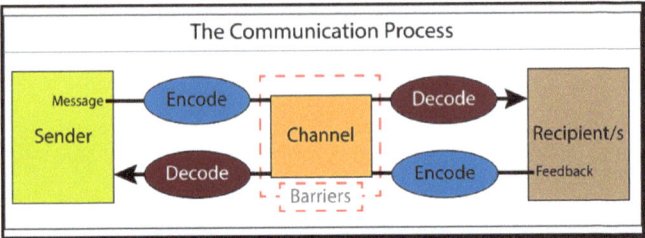

Retrieved from www.skillsyouneed.com

This reminds me of a complex flow chart or graphing sentences. But this is the true process of communication.

When you speak to someone, in any form, you are involving all parts of the process. Do you check for understanding? Is the message shared collectively? As you intended?

This is not going to be a lesson in formal communication skills or the process, there are thousands available. I am simply encouraging you to stop, pause, and reflect on what you say and do because it matters to those around you.

Part 2: Four Empowering Lessons About Connection

If you are not connecting, now is the perfect time to look inside, and see what needs to be adjusted. Take time to really see what your body language, posture, words, timing, tone, eye contact, and general demeanor say about you. Do you match your intent or what you hope others see? Are the two aligned?

If you are not sure, ask! Find someone you know, like, and trust, and ask them for feedback. But be prepared! It may not be what you want to hear. But on the other hand, you may be right in line.

So now is the time that you reflect on yourself and your interactions, on your inner light. Find your mirror and look at all the reflections while reflecting on you!

I can't wait to hear how you do! Find the good!

Share your stories at www.DoGoodLleadership.me

Part 2: Four Empowering Lessons About Connection

Part 2: Four Empowering Lessons About Connection

MY CHALLENGE TO YOU!

I encourage you to:

#1: Care and Connection

- be intentional with communication
- call a friend or family member
- write a note
- send an e-mail
- say hi to a stranger

#2: First Impressions

- hold the door open for a stranger
- say please and thank you
- make eye contact
- listen intently and ask questions

#3: The Impact of Words and Actions

- think before you speak
- really listen before responding

Part 2: Four Empowering Lessons About Connection

- choose the appropriate words
- monitor your tone
- note your facial expressions and body language

#4: Leaving a Legacy

- Did I provide a positive experience?
- Do I feel good about my interactions?
- Am I being a model for others?

Part 2: Four Empowering Lessons About Connection

THANK YOU!

I want to thank you for choosing this story to read. Out of the millions and millions of options, I'm honored that you chose Texas Angel Part 2. Be sure to also read Texas Angel Part 1 if you have not already done so.

I am honored you have decided to take the time to read stories about my amazing mom. I hope that you were able to connect and enjoy these true stories about her. She always made me smile along with thousands of others.

The life lessons in Texas Angel part 1 and the connection experiences in Texas Angel Part 2 are all derived from the positive memories I chose to highlight as I reflect on the life with my mom.

Of course, there were times when there were no smiles, there was frustration, anger, crying, and disappointment, but I choose to focus on the positive

Part 2: Four Empowering Lessons About Connection

times, the happy times, the ones that make me smile and laugh. Find the good!

She was not perfect, but she was caring, larger than life, and loved people. I hope you have experienced happiness while reading this. Perhaps you found a connection, or a particular story resonated with you.

I encourage you to reflect on your life, your interactions, those that influence you. What can you learn? How can you grow? What opportunities do you have to make a difference? Find the good! Be sure to look for my next book on reflection and finding the good. You won't want to miss it.

And if you are looking for a life coach to guide you towards more positivity, let's connect!

I help women, educators, and leaders realize their vivid vision through a positive metamorphosis and evolution to become a dynamic and motivating leader. If you are interested in joining my FREE Facebook page that

Part 2: Four Empowering Lessons About Connection

highlights growth, optimism, balance, and positive leadership through an *EMPOWERMENT EVOLUTION*, join today:

https://www.facebook.com/groups/dogoodleadership

Part 2: Four Empowering Lessons About Connection

Part 2: Four Empowering Lessons About Connection

WHAT'S NEXT?

1. Read *Texas Angel: Part 1*
2. Pick up the compilation of more than 800 family and friend recipes, *Recipes from a Texas Angel in Heaven*.
3. If you are interested in life coaching, let's connect!
4. If you are looking for a speaker for an event to share a program on communication, connection, positive leadership, or change, let's connect (see page 94-95)
5. If you are a woman, educator, or a leader and want to experience the Empowerment Evolution or are ready to transform your life through my Metamorphosis Method while becoming more confident and leading with intentionality and purpose, reach out on Facebook: https://www.facebook.com/groups/dogoodleadership
6. You may also visit my website! I would love to connect! www.DoGoodLeadership.me

Part 2: Four Empowering Lessons About Connection

One thing my mother always encouraged me to do was to follow my dreams. I am pursuing a personal goal of professional speaking, coaching, and training through Do Good Enterprises.

I would be honored if you would visit my website at: www.dogoodleadership.me

Part 2: Four Empowering Lessons About Connection

Part 2: Four Empowering Lessons About Connection

Speaking Programs

 Communication Connection: Just LEAD

Connecting through communication is a program that focuses on essential skill for effective customer service and instruction. The diversity of people today can require individualized approaches to communication. This program will highlight differences and insight to understanding yourself and those around you for effective communication. Just LEAD: Listen, Encourage, Ask questions, and Deliver.

 It's Time To SOAR

For any department or institution, it is essential that goal setting and planning takes place. It's Time to SOAR focuses on Simple Objectives, Ample Results to objectively and intentionally strategize a plan to implement systemically and successfully.

 Transformation with GRIT and Grace

It is essential that individuals are receptive to Transformation with GRIT and Grace. By using Goals, Resilience, Intention, and Time, one can find and feel success through the process of change. Although change can be uncomfortable and scary, by embracing and understanding the process, the results can be incredible.

 High Fives and Good Vibes: It's Time to RISE

In the world today, it is easy to get frustrated, procrastinate, and have a negative attitude toward yourself, your job, and those around you. This program will share strategies to 1) stop procrastinating, 2) start each day on a positive note, and 3) select one word that gives you purpose. It's time to RISE! Using Reflection and Introspection for Self-Empowerment (RISE). By having a positive attitude, daily challenges can be seen as opportunities, while frustration and isolation can turn into satisfaction and collaboration.

 Animal Essence Emulate, Replicate, and Formuate

Many times, we can relate our lives to those of animals. By studying how animals behave, interact, and communicate, individuals can Emulate, Replicate, and Formulate their own behaviors. Using a Panda Bear as a foundation, the program will share four animal behavior categories of interest for discussion and observation.

 Positive Leadership for Empowering Lives

Through the teachings of John Maxwell and Jon Gordon, it is known that positive leadership is essential now more than ever. Simply stated, a positive leader can make an insurmountable difference on a team, organization, and in the world. Through research and several examples that demonstrate the power of positive leadership, you will understand positive leadership models and approaches beginning with YOU! You have the power to elevate and empower those around you through Positive Leadership.

www.DoGoodLeadership.me

 601-669-6784   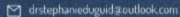 drstephanieduguid@outlook.com

Part 2: Four Empowering Lessons About Connection

If you are interested in downloading a FREE Goal Setting Workbook, follow the link here: https://www.gp.dogoodleadership.me/optin

Thank you for taking time to read *Texas Angel Part 2*.

Be sure to look for additional titles by Dr Stephanie Duguid on Amazon or visit

www.dogoodleadership.me.

www.ingramcontent.com/pod-product-compliance
Lightning Source LLC
Chambersburg PA
CBHW042305150426
43197CB00001B/17